The Urban Text

Mario Gandelsonas

LONGWOOD
LIBRARY

Longwood College, Farmville, Virginia 23901

A center for learning. A window to the world.

The Urban Text

Mario Gandelsonas

Essays by
Joan Copjec
Catherine Ingraham
John Whiteman

A Chicago Institute for Architecture and Urbanism Book
The MIT Press, Cambridge, Massachusetts and London, England

Chicago Institute for Architecture and Urbanism

Produced by the publications studio of the CIAU
Director of Publications: Richard Burdett
Graphic Designer: Mika Hadidian with Esterson Lackersteen
Typesetters: Opus Bureau, London, England
Printers: Balding and Mansell, Wisbech, England

© 1991 Mario Gandelsonas
Distributed by the MIT Press
Cambridge, Massachusetts and London, England

Library of Congress Cataloging–in–Publication Data
Gandelsonas, Mario, 1938 –
     The Urban Text / Mario Gandelsonas.
        p.   cm.

     ISBN 0 – 262 – 57084 – X (pbk.)
     1. City planning—Illinois—Chicago. 2. Architecture—Illinois—
—Chicago—Human factors. I. Title.
     NA9127. C4G36 1991
     711' .4'0977311—dc20   90–20883
                                   CIP

Acknowledgments
The material published in this book is part of ongoing research
developed over a number of years with the collaboration of
students in seminars and design studios. Here, I would like to
mention by name those whose support have been essential in
the development of this book.

    First, Diana Agrest, whose work in the theory and practice
of urbanism constitutes the point of departure of my research.

    John Whiteman, for making possible the development of
the computer drawings through a fellowship from the Chicago
Institute for Architecture and Urbanism.

    Bruce Graham, for his support and for suggesting the
use of the computer.

    Stanley Tigerman for his critical comments and for providing
the context at the School of Architecture, University of Illinois,
Chicago, where the two studios on Chicago took place.

    Julie Wheeler whose knowledge of the computer was
instrumental in the production of the drawings.

    There is a further debt to Richard Burdett for his editorial
advice and Mika Hadidian for the elegance of the layout and
design of this book.

MG

Contents

Photograph by Fritz Neumeyer

Linear Allusions   *Catherine Ingraham*

There is a moment in Claude Lévi-Strauss' book *Totemism,*[1] where, after a seemingly endless discussion of this and that theory of totemism, Lévi-Strauss enunciates a question that summarizes for me his whole argument about the structural analysis of culture. The question is, "Why all these birds?" It is through the examination of cultures which use bird totems in particularly interesting ways that Lévi-Strauss is able to unravel the "totemic illusion." But it is the form of the question that interests me and I want to use it here to talk about Mario Gandelsonas' work. This is perhaps not as inappropriate a suggestion as it might at first seem since Gandelsonas has undertaken something very close to a structural analysis of the American city. My question is, "Why all these lines?"

For there is clearly at work, in what Gandelsonas calls the "architecturalizing of the city," a concern with lines. These linear maps suggest that one is able to read the deep structure of the city through extracted linear structures – streets, avenues, grids, figure/ground reversals, housing blocks. This idea, in itself, is not new. It typifies in a general way how most city planners, urbanists and architects have read/drawn the city in this century. What is unusual about Gandelsonas' work – and the structural import it might have for American urbanism in particular – is the way in which his studies reflect on their own linear strategy. In the midst of an almost classical urban analysis, Gandelsonas adds a twist to the lines, or outlines, of the city. At first, this looks like a topographical twist where the non-linear shapes of rivers and lakes interrupt the neat dominance of the Jeffersonian grid. But this topographical twist is only substituting for what I want to call an architectural twist, a substitution I will try to elucidate in this essay.

Gandelsonas has likened the architect's gaze to Freud's floating attention of the analyst. The architect/urbanist looks with a floating gaze at the city's "data" in order to grasp some central fact about the city's morphology and ideology. While the architect's gaze is first hypnotized by the regularity of the grid, it soon finds the failures of the grid more provocative, as charged as jokes in psychoanalysis. But one cannot escape the fact that this attention, however fortuitous its observations, ultimately must find a way to make use of its material. One might say that while the attention is wandering, it is in the interest of the line (whose systems are antithetical to wandering) to redouble its hold. It is in the recidivism of analyst and patient both – the relapse into sense-making – that we see where and how the line has exercised a certain control from the beginning.

The idea of the line as I have just used it here, its will to power, its competition with the raw romanticism of a drifting analysis, is an idea of a wilful and ideal technicity. The technical, like the military, always appears on stage in the uniform of law, order and clarity. Its role is to provide the constraints within which all-too-human actors (possessed of ambiguous psyches and dis-orderly costumed bodies) must work and struggle. But, as we shall see, this drama of opposition that the order of the line stages does not hold up. One might say that the uniformed figure of the technical retains its power only so long as one does not see it as yet another costume, as possibly the costume of the fool or jester.

But let us say, for the moment, that this technical drama does hold up. Am I suggesting that Gandelsonas' technical and linear vocabulary – a vocabulary of the computer, the printer, the grid – keeps the American cities he studies "in line" in a way that makes the "floating attention" an impossibility? My answer is yes and no. Gandelsonas seems, himself, to be aware of the competition between the technical and its "other" – however one might style that "other." His work might even be said to cultivate this confrontation. Indeed, if this work can instruct us, as I believe it can, in how to analyse the city "architecturally," then part of that instruction will have to do with the control that the line (and linear apparatus) exerts on the project and the slippage of that control both within the project and the linear apparatus itself.

1 C Lévi-Strauss, *Totemism* (Boston, 1963)

The reason I was able to answer "yes and no" to the question of whether the city is kept in line by Gandelsonas' computer drawings, is because of a paradox that is written into the idea of the line itself. As Derrida has remarked "the enigmatic model of the line was the very thing that philosophy could not see when it had its eyes open on the interior of its own history. This night begins to lighten a little at the moment when linearity – which is not loss or absence but the repression of pluri-dimensional symbolic thought – relaxes its oppression because it begins to sterilize the technical and scientific economy that it has long favored."[2] When the line, and the linear economy it devises, tries to set itself up as an indispensable technical or scientific tool – as the best and most efficient path through materiality or conceptuality – it sterilizes itself and the path as a site of signification. For signification and meaning are irreducibly pluri-dimensional and cannot live in a single-dimensional ideality. The line undoes itself at the very moment that it asserts its linear control most strongly. Thus even as certain linear apparatuses (not only computer drawings, but also statistical charts and diagrams) are marshalled to organize city data into a technical economy, the significance of this economy has escaped into other regions – regions hostile to and disruptive of the line's hegemony. Thus Gandelsonas' project seems built up out of the opportunities provided by the drift of the lines it produces. The project breaks into the mythology of the technical that his machine of composition, the computer, is dedicated to keeping inviolate.

The computer acts as a storehouse and keeper of the line. To begin with it keeps the linear mark intact regardless of how much that mark is beleaguered by the addition of new marks. Computer-generated lines can simulate ambiguity but none of this ambiguity contaminates the system of generation. Provided one knows the appropriate commands, one can always reverse the build-up of complexity and return to the first line or the first point, to the coordinates. In many respects, the computer is able to retain the line as a clean mark because it sees the line as two-dimensional, possessing length and breadth but not depth. Intersections between lines are not a build-up of graphic material but of the superimposition of two planes that never quite touch. One can see very quickly in the computer both the corroboration and failure of Euclidean ideals. The computer must simulate all the geometric rules we are familiar with from Euclid and yet the graphic demonstration of these rules always stops short. Nothing can ever fully intersect, in the computer, to produce a new element (as in the production of a line through the intersection of planes in Euclid). One can always recover what has been stored away. But this recovery is neither a rereading nor an act of history. Instead it is a starting over in the most banal sense of the term. The promiscuity of the manually drawn or printed line, its tendency to enlarge and disperse under observation, is muted and controlled by the computer.

Now when the architect/planner uses the computer to represent the city, he/she confronts a system that, while available to linear representation, does not belong in any direct sense to a linear realm. The grid, the avenue, the horizon line are not stored in the city as retrievable properties or even as discernible coordinate points. The section (map or plan) must be dissected out of a series of complex layers that (as Le Corbusier in particular noted) are resistant to this surgery. Traditionally, these sections or nodes have been selected according to the hierarchy offered by monumental structures, key axes, prominent topographical features. Gandelsonas' computer reading of the city is neither hierarchical in this traditional sense – although it has moments of hierarchy – nor is it a simple mapping of what "merely exists." It is, instead, the tracing of a refractory path between the sterilizing line of the computer and the fertile line of the city – which we might liken to refracting the exterior structure of the line (the Euclidean ideal that the computer strives for) through the interior structure of the line (the graphic, territorial, topographical lines

2 J Derrida, *Of Grammatology*, tr. G Chakravorty Spirak (Baltimore and London, 1976), p. 86.

that possess dimension). Or, since this is certainly enigmatic, we might liken it to refracting the idealized economy of the machine through the dream or trace economy of the city. The act of refraction – a deflection of the line as it leaves one medium, the computer, and enters another, the city, or vice versa – results in a series of straight, but minutely disconnected, lines. The "method," if there is one, is as lawless as any other method. But I think Gandelsonas' method, to a certain degree, feels its own lawlessness.

Gandelsonas' "desire to describe" (his own words) these cities is not a desire for paraphrastic description – that is, description that walks alongside the city (or the map of the city) and points out the sights. It is, instead, a descriptive power that possesses a "middle register" – a register that can both occupy the traditional city and yet read it in a new way. Gandelsonas is not interested, as he might have been, with Derrida's concern for a history of the city and the architectural narration of its stages, text by text, context by context, demonstrating the economy that each time imposes graphic disorder. Instead, he attempts a form of description that assembles different threads and lines of meaning, putting them, as it were, on the same plane – a plane where none of these threads or lines really feel at home. The plane has a certain dark aesthetic, and it is clearly a territory produced by ink. It is a densely written-upon territory but it has the substance of a dream narrative. The scribe/describer, Gandelsonas, simply tells, and thus interprets, the dream as he remembers it. "First," he might say, "I moved this grid to the left. Then I moved it up a bit. Then I discovered this bizarre space and I concentrated on that." To this dream narrative, the analyst, also Gandelsonas, responds in kind by giving the dream a structure – not a cause/effect structure, but an analogic structure. "This space" the analyst might say, "resembles another space over here, so what do you make of that, etc." In this banal interchange (the banality of it is precisely the point) the bringing into one plane, the making linear, of a mingled set of events – figures, images, dreams, texts, architectures, "the real city," "the fantastical city" – becomes an analytic opportunity.

Let me briefly take up what this opportunity could be. Its structural character is certainly analogic, but each analogy must find its analytic power within the linear picture produced by the computer. I notice, for example, three such analogic "figures" in Gandelsonas' drawings of Chicago: the serpent/tree/river, the grid, and an almost-assembled, or almost destroyed, structure, perhaps a house.

The serpent – how tiresome but endlessly interesting the serpent is. Here is a figure of linearity gone really bad. Here is the creature that tempted Eve to the transgression of the garden, to the breaking of the pastoral domesticity subsisting between herself and Adam. She was tempted into the urbanistic, the non-rural city of knowledge and the problems of duplicitous language – lying, masking, figurative speech and, in the nomenclature of the garden, evil. The grid is our Cartesian inheritance, the flawed restoration of the uprightness, the elevational, that the serpent already knew about and disputed, as much with its body as with its sly rhetoric. But how are these figures – clever as they are – to be used? What is the urbanistic lesson, if any? How can the lines of demarcation between one section of a city and the next – lines that sometimes happen to coincide in Gandelsonas' drawings with lines of racial or economic division – be said to interact with their two-dimensional morphology? Let me yield, for the moment, to the allure of these images (for we have been speaking of Freud). Here the city becomes the site of differences between plan (that which lies flat) and elevation (that which stands up). The serpent, in plan, finds a kinship with the topography – describing the path of rivers and coastlines – while, in elevation, it becomes a branching tree (I am looking, in particular, at the computer images of the Chicago River, see – for example – page 29). The topographical serpent climbs, and in climbing runs into the very thing that it will need as a instrument of persuasion, the tree of knowledge. Thus does Eve, who lives in the delimited and walled house of Eden, see that the serpent has the power to negotiate the difference between the horizontal and the vertical. This is certainly a fearful kind of sexual negotiation, for it makes the serpent morphologically hermaphroditic. The analogic figure of this kind of hermaphroditic morphology is, of course, architecture which also negotiates between plan and elevation. Thus one can make the move from the figure of the serpent/tree/river to an architectural figure that thematizes the non-linearity of the path from architectural plan to elevation, an observation that might have a certain prescriptive value in city planning. It might be objected that an analogic attention would allow us to make any move whatsoever – and that all moves are therefore suspect. But, in fact, while Gandelsonas' drawings (or any drawings for that matter) may be hypothetically interpreted in an infinite variety of ways, there are only a few readings that the horizon of his project actually supports. It is only, one might say, fantasies that have urbanistic or architectural import that we are interested in here.

The serpent story – only a story to be sure – is a story about the difference between plan and elevation. It is, then, potentially a story about the difference between the American city as a modernist phenomenon (pocked with the large plazas and plinths that arose directly out of a plan/elevation relationship advocated by modern architecture) and the city as a structural or post-structural entity. It is potentially a story about social and political difference – refracted through the paradigm of gender difference. And, further, it is potentially a story about the urban "house," the relation of topography to architecture, the meaning of the "boundary" and "district." These stories do not allow one to look at either architecture, or urbanism, in quite the same way. One can no longer even draw the city in quite the same way – as Gandelsonas' work most profoundly shows. All of these stories open up an architectural moment in the midst of the city that is neither the individual building, the housing district, the commercial corridor. Instead, it is a middle register of analysis that releases the geometric line (computerized in this case) into the city, as one might release an animal from its cage. This is not a full release, but a further act of design and architecture, since the line only wanders into another shape, another structure. But the difference is that these shapes and structures do not offer themselves as new objects, or new urban plans, but as opportunities for bringing into play an immense range of hidden material – sometimes fantastical material – which, of course, is what the city drama, and the architectural drama, is all about.

The Grid and the Logic of Democracy   *Joan Copjec*

One of the most comical displays of television's stubborn resistance to sophisticated thought was that medium's often repeated battle with what it called the "Teflon President." Every blunder, every lie that was caught by the camera was played and replayed on the nightly news, juxtaposed to an image which directly contradicted, and thus exposed, the falsity of the President's words. But though by this means it could decisively refute one statement after another, the medium could not – by its own incredulously tendered admission – menace the position of the President himself. Ronald Reagan emerged virtually unscathed by all these proofs of the incompetence and mendacity of his speech.

What television did not realize, of course, was that the audience was repeating – in a peculiar, twentieth-century way – the gesture of a very famous seventeenth-century philosopher: René Descartes. Television thus blinded itself to the precise fact which that gesture revealed – that there is an instance (linguistic theory calls it the enunciating instance) that exceeds all the enunciations or statements any subject may make. The subject (or, in Descartes' terms, the cogito) *is*, in fact, this enunciating instance. Descartes argued that even if every thought one thought, every statement one uttered could be doubted, could be shown to be guilty of some error or deception, the *instance* of doubt – of thought or speech – could not be doubted: it remained innocent of all charges of error.

By continuing to believe in the President, then, even as it grew more and more suspicious of what the President said, i.e., by believing in the enunciator while doubting the enunciations, the American television audience demonstrated its access to Cartesian philosophy. Now, this claim may appear to you wild and unsubstantiative, but only if you fail to see that Descartes is, in a sense, the father of democracy; only if you fail to realize that the American revolution could not have taken place without him. For no-one would have thought of fighting for the rights of a pure,

denatured, universal subject – a subject whose value is not determined by race, creed, color, sex or station in life – no-one would have thought of waging a war on behalf of liberty and justice for all subjects, if Descartes had not already isolated for us this pure, abstract instance in whose name the war would be waged: the democratic subject, devoid of characteristics. This is surely the source of America's self-proclaimed "radical innocence," this belief in a basic humanity in which this nation's diverse citizens share. There is, then, at least according to this logic, nothing surprising in the phenomenon of the Teflon President. An American public made sentimental about the flag, redoubled its belief in the fundamental democratic principle for which it stands. Reagan, who stirred up this sentiment, became the emblematic repository, the most visible beneficiary of this increase of belief.

But what, you may be asking yourself, does such an analysis have to do with architecture? What, by this roundabout means, is being introduced into the discourse? The subject of psychoanalysis. For psychoanalysis, like Descartes, also posits an instance beyond speech, an instance with no positive characteristics. Now, of all the things to which architectural discourse has remained resistant, psychoanalysis is certainly one of the most notable. Perhaps this is why the French psychoanalyst Jacques Lacan always seemed to me to be addressing architects specifically when he warned: you don't have to know the plan of a building in order to bang your head against its walls. As a matter of fact, it is precisely through your ignorance that you guarantee such accidents. Architecture may very well continue to ignore psychoanalysis and the unconscious, but this will only ensure that the unconscious will continue to bedevil architecture: just as the television campaign described above was bedevilled by the persistence of the Cartesian subject.

What can it mean to say that architecture – without knowing it – continuously bangs its head against the unconscious?

To illustrate, let us focus on the example of the ubiquitous grid plan of American cities. No-one who knows nothing of psychoanalysis, I would argue, can adequately understand the insistence of this grid. Again, this will seem an extravagant claim: a great deal is known of the rationale and history of this type of city plan. We know, for example, about the Hippodamian method by which Miletus, Olynthus, Priene and other ancient Greek cities were laid out in a way that seemed to structure them according to classical ideas of beauty and order. Some have been tempted to speculate that a relation between the grid and democracy is already established here, in this earlier moment. But such speculation can lead nowhere, for it proceeds from an a-historical perspective and fails to take cognizance of the fact that modern democracy is not reducible to a form of government, as it was in classical times. Modern democracy is a much broader phenomenon; it defines the entire social field, the system of social relations that tie us to and cordon us off from others. It defines the very structure of the modern subject.

If we are to respect the historical specificity of the gridiron construction of American cities, we would be better advised to look to Thomas Jefferson rather than the elusive Hippodamus – but only if we bear in mind the point we have already argued: that it was Descartes who was the father of the "father of American democracy." When he passed the Land Ordinance of 1785, which called for the generalization and extension of the chess-board divisions and subdivisions of Eastern cities over the Western territories, Jefferson was engaging in a radical act of Cartesian disincorporation. Sweeping away any and all natural or subjective particulars by which America – the "melting pot," the "nation of immigrants"– might otherwise begin to define itself, he submitted the country to a universal quantifier: the grid. The territories came to be defined as part of our nation, as American, not through a marking out and celebration of their peculiar geographic features, but through an erasure of all such features. Similarly, if all our citizens can be said to be Americans, this is not because we share any positive characteristics, but rather because we have all been given the right to *shed* these characteristics. It is this right, granted by the Constitution – this equality of condition, this right to appear disembodied before the law – that constitutes us as citizens of the USA. I divest myself of positive identity, therefore I am an American. This is the peculiar logic of democracy.

It is also, as is plain, a paradoxical logic. At a seminar held at the Chicago Institute for Architecture and Urbanism, where Mario Gandelsonas' "Urban Text" project was under discussion, one of the most interesting points of disagreement concerned the legibility of the city space defined by the grid. There was among the participants of the seminar no consensus of opinion about whether the regular and systematic disposition of streets, the standardization of their relations: 1) logicizes space, and thus renders it clearly intelligible, or 2) creates a monotonous sameness that detracts from the space's intelligibility. The indecision of the seminar recapitulated many of the arguments made about the paradoxes of democracy in general. Democracy is the only social system in which every individual has a chance to express his or her particular will, every individual has a vote that counts. The paradox is that it only counts as one, as an abstract statistic. The individual's particularity is thus annulled by the very act of its expression. Examples could be multiplied, but the point is already clear – democracy simultaneously presides over the rise of the bourgeois individual and his or her anonymity; the modern individual is also the "man lost in a crowd."

But what is more problematic than this paradox are the misguided attempts to resolve it. Since the problem is perceived as anonymity, since it is the resoluteness of individual identity which is imagined to be in jeopardy under democracy, it is thought that individuality must be restored and safeguarded through a retreat of the law. To avoid suffocating the individual, the law must withdraw and allow – or, better, enable and guarantee – each citizen to express himself freely. This very argument has been advanced in support of the grid, for those who support its deployment usually praise it as the least restrictive means of organizing a city. The grid neither legislates nor limits the sort of building or activity that will occupy any particular segment of the city; the spaces it designates are free to develop in a variety of ways. The grid merely coordinates spaces and thus provides one space with access to all the others.

Alexis de Tocqueville is one of the best-known critics of this modern notion of a tutelary form of government, of a "mild and provident" law. He feared that it could easily be combined with an entirely new and very dangerous form of servitude. One imagines that in looking into the future of "democracy in America," Tocqueville somehow caught a glimpse of that inane yellow circle with the eyes and smiling mouth that is often accompanied by the ethical imperative: "Have a nice day!" I cite this latest, popular emblem of our mild and provident principle of law not to trivialize it, but rather to indicate more clearly what, in essence, in distilled form, it commands: happiness. Now, what could be wrong with that?

Happiness is, alas, structurally impossible. Since psychoanalysis has provided us with our only account of this impossibility, it is to its analysis that we turn to help us theorize the relation between happiness and democracy. What, in fact, is *Totem and Taboo,* if not this very theorization? In this work – his favorite, we are told – Freud constructs a modern myth about sons who rise up and kill their father. The inherited myth of Oedipus no longer seems useful and Freud feels compelled to invent his own, one which tells of the historical surpassing of Oedipus. What tale is this if not that of the mythical origins of democracy? For, once the father – Oedipus – is murdered, that is, once the king and the whole monarchical system of inherited knowledge and power are destroyed, the brothers, thus freed, establish a fraternity of equals, a democracy. There is, however, one problem. While the brothers had thought that the murder of the father would remove him as the external impediment to their enjoyment of the women in the horde, it turns out that the guilt incurred by the murder severely prohibits their enjoyment. The father, in death (i.e., as super-ego), proves to be more powerful as a privative force than he was in life.

What does this myth tell us about democracy? It warns that there is one right which cannot be equally distributed to all. One right resists universalization: the right to enjoyment, to *jouissance.* This does not mean that there is no harm in trying, that we should applaud those who "have their hearts in the right place" and who display their democratic fervor by working toward the distribution of the greatest good to the greatest number. Happiness is not simply a futile goal, it is a dangerous one, for this reason: the exception of *jouissance* from the list of universalizable rights is the condition of the possibility of the universalization of the others. It is only *because* the dead father retains a surplus of *jouissance* that the brothers are able to form a society of equals; their society is constituted precisely through their *privation.* It is on the basis of their lack, of what they do not have, that their equality is founded. There can be no better definition of democracy than this. Democracy is that modern social form that dispenses with all positive supports – the body of the king, the tradition of ancestors, scientific assertions of truth. It is only the absence of guarantees that guarantees democracy. I doubt therefore I am, the Cartesian dictum, is the very formula for democracy. With this difference: while Descartes considered the cogito the source, democracy must be defined as the precipitate of doubt.

By definition, then, democracy is an unsettling, a conflictual space; it is therefore undermined by liberal attempts to reduce this conflict, it is destroyed by the valorization and encouragement of pluralism, i.e., of a plurality of positive and peacefully coexisting differences. Although such a Utopia is often presented as the goal of democracy, history and psychoanalysis have made it clear that striving after this goal leads inexorably to the subversion of democratic principles, the evaporation of the only basis on which democracy can be founded. The attempt to secure the peaceful coexistence of all entails a surrendering of doubt for the proleptic certainty of the whole, the whole *within* which differences would presumably take their place and *to* which they would become subservient. In fact, this peaceful coexistence can never be achieved, will never happen, and this subservience that Tocqueville presciently feared – the product of a modern form of law, kinder and gentler than any encountered before – has in this century already unleashed a sort of horror unimaginable before the modern era.

What sort of law, then, can we expect to *conserve* democracy, to maintain the markers of uncertainty which would forbid our ever fully recognizing ourselves in our fellow citizens? For it is only when I am willing to grant rights to the other who is *not* like me that I can truly be considered democratic. Only psychoanalysis has been able systematically to formulate this law of democracy and it has done so precisely by defining, and insisting on, the limit of universalization. According to psychoanalysis, the Cartesian method of doubt always fails to rid thought completely of all its "pathological" (in Kant's sense) contents. Some excess pathological product is always produced as a residue of this method; this product is doubt itself. This ineliminable uncertainty prohibits our ever being able totally to comprehend ourselves or others. Something remains unavailable to us, unconscious. This remainder, the unconscious in which we can never recognize ourselves, *is* the social bond in a democracy. The law of psychoanalysis, then, is never simply provident but always also privative; it includes, in other words, its own negation.

The grid – as the urban law of democracy – is similarly conflictual; it comports within itself its own transgression, its own limit or exception. The grid is not, contrary to the way it is ordinarily conceived, infinitely extensible, in principle limitless. The breaks in the gridplan are not resistances to it, points at which another, external force – nature, financial, political, or ethnic – will transgress its law. The breaks are internal to and not transgressions of the grid. Broadway – or some such exception – is always structurally necessary to the functioning of this democratic law. Through his analysis of the transgressive law of the American city grid, Mario Gandelsonas has rendered an account of the formation of the urban unconscious – in order to allow architects to stop banging their heads against it.

Read Me If You Can?   *John Whiteman*

Just looking

I am holding one of Mario Gandelsonas' computer drawings of Chicago (see page 81). He has told me that it is taken from a map of the Chicago Loop. I easily recognize this, and indeed can point to familiar streets and quickly find the locations of favorite buildings, such as Inland Steel and the Harris Bank. From the reduced information that is presented to me cartographically I can reconstruct in my mind, with the aid of memory, what I think to be a complete picture or version of the "real" city. All drawings are samples, I remember: if an urban drawing were to be complete, it would be a city, or at least the size of a city, and so not a drawing. I know therefore that somehow my own sense and feelings must act as a go-between from the limitations of the drawing to the plenitude of the city.

I notice, however, something else in my reactions. I am responding to the drawing not just as a map, but also in some other, more elusive way. Amid, indeed in the very heart of the drawing's seemingly accurate delineations, I notice the careful movement of a contrived design. I quickly realize that subtly, almost imperceptibly, Chicago has been idealized in this drawing. There are very fine discrepancies between what is represented in the drawing and what I know to be the case in the city itself. Large blocks of the Loop are not quite where they are supposed to be, and indeed are plucked out in the drawing almost as figure. North-South streets have been given a strange emphasis which differentiates them from East-West streets in a way that is more than just an encoding of the difference which I find in the city itself. Indeed the overall sense of the city's orthogonality has been heightened, almost cartooned in over-emphasis. Some blocks, which I know not to exist, have been drawn in with the intention of completing an immanent pattern. The pattern of alleys has been idealized. I realize that I cannot take the drawing as literally as it seems at first to suggest itself.

Just dreaming

I cease to look at the drawing's particulars with reference to the city that I know, and I start looking at them only in relation to the total structure of the drawing itself. Indeed I forget all about the Chicago with which I am familiar, and I meander only in the confines of the drawing, playing this shape off against that, watching how this white line cuts its way through that particular density of black drawing. I begin to have feelings which are generated by mechanisms other than reference or depiction; mechanisms which, because they are without any direct means of reference, seem to entrance me in a purely formalist reading of the drawing. I do not need to know, so it seems, what every piece of the drawing is, to what it corresponds in reality. I need only to watch how individual pieces of the drawing move against each other in the overall configuration, and how in this movement they gain their identities as individual pieces of a drawing.

I am attending to the drawing's evocations, to what it expresses. Expression achieves its effects, seems magical, because no direct line of reference can be traced from the sign and its configuration to the meaning. Instead of a direct line of reference, expression engages in a movement or circuit of meaning. Caught up by this movement, much in the way that a breath of wind may take up the sail of a boat, I see the city reconfigured. It swarms before my eyes in a strange play of shapes, and appears as unstable and as unintelligible as any dream.[1]

But, as in all dreams my sense of fantasy and freedom is not what it seems. The dream is profoundly the position of someone who does not see, of one who is blinded. The movement of my dream is only made against and therefore is constrained within the authority of the city's grid. This constraint has the effect of haunting any fantasia which I would construct from the drawing, much in the way that the daily anxieties of life haunt the dreams of persons in the patterns of ordinary sleep. Reality exerts its rude

---

1 Mario Gandelsonas appeals explicitly to Freud's method of reading errors as symptoms in order to explain the method of his drawings of Chicago. See S Freud, *The Interpretation of Dreams* (New York, 1955). Gandelsonas looks for the dominant pattern in Chicago's urban form, (i.e., the grid), and then against an idealized version of the actual grid he reads all the exceptions and idiosyncrasies of the street patterns as symptoms. But as symptoms of what? We are only shown, never told.

presence again, or rather I acknowledge that the apparent release or pure freedom of the dream is a fantasy made over and against the continued and unabated authority of urban regulation.

My feelings, constructed from the drawing, are fully hostage, I realize, to the regulations of the city from which in dreaming I have apparently escaped. More to the point, the drawing and I are both still subject to the urban formation in which this scene takes place. Indeed my pleasure in the drawing is in part produced by the (re)presentation, indeed the over-emphasis of the strictures of the city in which I am actually standing, even (especially) as I look at a drawing which purports to represent it.

My fantasia is not then a pure wilderness, not a pure leave of the senses, but a wilderness that has been channelled and routed, haunted with the ghost of long, straight streets seeking the horizon of the city in the landscape that barely can be glimpsed in the space beyond.

Thinking out loud

Suddenly a theorist taps me on the shoulder. Jolted back to a world full of questions, I begin by asking if I can relate the sensations of my fantasia, a scene in which the city at first had been forgotten, back to the reality of the city which had prompted my excursions in the first place, and which had re-exerted itself in the dream. In short, I am asking myself if indeed I can read the drawing that I hold in my hands. After all, it is only a computer printout: how hard can it be? Can we not call a street a "street", and a block a "block"?

Well, perhaps, despite the convolution of expression, there is difficulty involved. I know already that the sensations I wish to explain seem at first to deny any literal or direct relation to the real city, so called. I am doomed to provide an account of

a reference from drawing to city that is at best indirect. Perhaps it is a route that cannot be charted by the familiar plan of determination running from name ("block") to picture (rectangle) to urban element (block). (The relay of name-image-thing is still a dominant mechanism for securing the referents of words, for the construction of sense.) Still, having read too much analytic philosophy, and being one who prefers mystery to mysticism, I set about my task armed with a heavy dose of English scepticism, relishing the prospect of a little iconoclasm.

I retreat immediately to my library. I pull the relevant texts by Freud from the shelf, so that I can corroborate Gandelsonas' own statements about his drawings being somehow concerned with "the unconscious of the city", and I pick up my copy of Rossi's *The Architecture of the City*, because I remember him writing about the autonomy of artifacts, an idea that may seem at first to challenge any contention to read and hence find "meaning" in such things as cities, buildings or drawings.[2] I sit down to ask first whether I was warranted in reading the drawings in a way more complex than the literal. Subsequently, and more importantly, the first question still lingering unanswered in my mind, I try to understand what I can theorize concerning the difficulty of this task.

The morning light of theory

Since Aldo Rossi so forcefully drew our attention to the brute fact of the city as material artifact, we have had to live with the problem of the city in a different way. Once it was thought that the form of the city would appear in our minds as a necessary conclusion to problems stated with the clarity and purpose of the social sciences. Urban form would not have to be designed; it could be deduced from social theory. The artifact of the city was thought to be purely instrumental, material form being a

2 A Rossi, *The Architecture of the City* (Cambridge, 1982), Chapter 1, "The Structure of Urban Artifacts," pp. 29-61.

frictionless conduit, offering no complexities of translation, no resistance and no other avenues of possibilities to our social purposes abstractly conceived. In Rossi's straw man of "naive functionalism" we had a model of thinking in which urban form seemed to cancel out of human interests, playing no significant role in and of itself.[3]

Rossi's urban theories changed all this. He pointed out the obvious but forgotten fact that material formations, such as cities and buildings, often persist beyond the time scale of any single regime of human interest or form of life. Even if the material of building or city is demolished, certain features of its geometry are pathologically preserved in any new construction on the site of the old. Rossi pointed to events such as the Roman amphitheatre at Arles being absorbed into the housing fabric of the mediaeval city; and he asked questions with such points as, "How can the same geometrical form be deduced from a social description of the 'entertaining' slaughter of wild beasts and men and also from a description of medieval housing needs or customs"? Surely, he concluded, the geometry of buildings and cities was not so unequivocal as the "naive functionalist" would have us believe.[4]

Rossi's famous reparation of this yawning gap in functionalist thinking was to describe and stress the autonomy of the form and artifacts of the city. He showed how the material form of cities and buildings had a life of its own, and seemed to persist like a thread of platinum through all the changing circumstances of the ancient and modern world. Cities and buildings do not fit human lives as a glove fits a hand, he concluded, but rather must be thought to have a more judicious relation to the play of human interests in a collective pattern such as the city.

The relation of form to life cannot be opened up as an incurable gap in the way that functionalist arguments suppose: that there is, on the one hand, innocuous material in which form is constituted, material which is in some originary state devoid of significance, and on the other something called life which is replete with the play of significance but, for the purposes of design, devoid of form. We know from Rossi that this formula is full of faults, however logical it may appear; and that form and life are inconceivable the one without the other. Thus the relation between the two cannot be reduced to an instrumental formula. Urban formations will always involve design and complex judgement: urban design is necessarily judicious.[5]

Neglecting the socialist thinking which is only just below the surface of Rossi's writing, avoiding the long shadow of historical materialism, many architects in the United States have taken Rossi's arguments for the formal autonomy of cities and buildings as a license to drop all social concern in architectural practice. Better to be realistic about the fact that architecture is a practice which always takes place in the close embrace of power: and what better rationalization of an autonomous practice (falsely considered) can one find than an argument that secures the autonomy of the profession's concerns?

But this was not Rossi's point at all. He did not wish to break the relation between material form and cultural meaning. He wished only to avoid short-circuiting or misconstruing it. Instead he wished to acknowledge the full difficulty of the relation, thereby making it more powerful not less, retrieving not severing a culturally significant practice for the architect. His was only an argument against treating material form as a mere illustration for a social theory which would purport to explain and determine it. It was not an argument against the cultural relevance of form itself. Indeed it was the reverse.

Thus deprived of any direct cross-walk between descriptions of our social interests and the material form of our urban existence, we have been in search of new explanations and new practices of urbanism.

3 Rossi, *ibid.*, pp. 46-48.
4 Rossi, *ibid.*, pp. 57-61.
5 Rossi, *ibid.*

Drawing as a third term

Curiously then, Rossi's theories bring me to a similar impasse as my analysis of my own reactions to Gandelsonas' drawings. In the former I reject any direct relation between city form and urban life: in the latter I denounce any direct relation between drawing and city. Yet in each case I am anxious also to deny the absence of a relation.

Logically I could spare myself a lot of trouble were I prepared to say that no concept of a relation is needed. I could say that the issue is one of an unrecognized, perhaps suppressed identity: that life might be identified with its material forms; and that the city might be no more than its representations. There is clearly some appeal to this, for when a drawing is expressive we are often prepared to say that its connection to reality is more and not less direct than a literal reference between the depicting and the depicted, for any sense of a gap between the two, depicting and depicted, appears to have been closed down. The drawing passes over into its subject without any sense of distance between two entities. Expression is associated therefore with a more intimate and immediate sense of knowing than mediated routes of reference, such as denotation and diagram.[6]

But the concept of an identity will not solve my puzzle, for it also excludes the middle ground of play, the sense of a space in which, for example, the city is constantly evoked by its representations and the two are also revised against each other.

In an alternate conception the drawing may enter the space between form and life, not as an entity opposed to either one of its poles, but as a third term (among other third terms, such as language or the persistence of cultural rhythm). As such the drawing also enters the city, not as something independent from it, but as something in play with it and also as a part of it. Each drawing is at once a condensation of certain senses of the city, but also a reaching out to the city itself: a drawing away from and simultaneously a drawing towards. John Dewey has characterized this double-sensed relation as "an alembic"[7] – the process of distillation of alcohol extracts from grain, which, in conjunction with other ingredients and the use of a still forms a new liquid; but the taste of this liquid is at once the taste of whiskey and also the taste of the Scottish summer, of the long days of rain and sunshine, of lingering light on warm evenings when the sun hangs low on the horizon, when people walk in the landscape casting shadows fully half the length of football fields, when the perfume of heather on the hills fills the damp night air. All this and more is distilled from the flora of grain, and put into casks which are then stored underground for a decade or more.

Such is also the relation between drawing and city: the drawing is a distillation of urban qualities into a new site, the site of the drawing itself. The drawing thus appears to be at once intimate and distant from its subject. Certain of Mario Gandelsonas' computer drawings do indeed function in this manner. As such they appear as mediation between the form of the city and the flow of life within it. I imagine such mediating entities as a third term in the opposition of form and life, invoking all the neutralities and mystique of the third as a supplement to the pair, the opposed duality.

Drawing and urban design

Acknowledging such entities and developing a skill with them is crucial in the development of the practice of urban design. The city itself, either in un-edited part or in its entirety, cannot be made the object of a designer's attention: such samples of the city cannot be covered by the scope of a single design action. This is too much to do: the city as such cannot be bent to the human will. But as yet, architects have not been able to formulate a concept of urban design which is not predicated on instrumental control in

6 N Goodman, "The Sound of Pictures," *Languages of Art* (Cambridge, 1976), Chapter 2, pp. 52-53.

7 J Dewey, "The Expressive Object," *Art and Experience* (New York, 1980), Chapter 5, p. 82 .

design. Lacking such control, urban design is too often thought to be futile, largely because one cannot trust the play of judgement. However, these drawings by Mario Gandelsonas can break this impasse without backtracking on the hard-learned lessons of Aldo Rossi. Rossi too was anxious to avoid the false totalizations of instrumental control and also to acknowledge the apparent independence of material form in the flow of city life. Drawings such as these by Gandelsonas offer an alternative, for they stand in the way between the form of the city and the pattern of its real interests. As such they are opaque.

In discussions of urban design they might function or be used in a number of ways, positive and negative. (I shall limit myself to suggesting but a few such uses here: I do not intend to be exhaustive.) First, the drawing may act as an alternate object in debates of urban development, almost as a surrogate for the city itself: as if the consequences of a projected action appear not only in the city but also in another guise, in the drawing. The two projections of design consequences, the one against the city proper, the other against the city as (re)drawn, can then be played off against each other, providing the material for comparison and judgement. Designs can be projected contingently with a greater sense of consequence. Second, the drawing may revise the city itself. It may, in being marginally unrealistic, elucidate forms that are immanent in the existing urban fabric, thus guiding the imagination of development. Both these are positive functions of the drawing in urban design. There is one final role for the drawing, however, which is not predicated on such a positive view of urban improvement.

Finally, the drawing may actually enter the city, and act as a thesaurus from which senses of the city can be retrieved at a later date. The process of development is rarely as considered as it might be, and the identity of a city, while persisting, may seem at times to disappear. The urban drawing may function at times as a vault in which a fuller life of the city is preserved as in death, to be revived as in a dream, when the imagination takes its flight. The function of drawing as storing, one might say.

The Urban Text *Mario Gandelsonas*

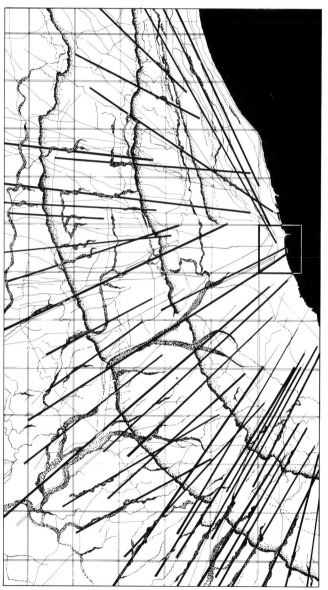

Analytic drawing of Chicago in its territorial context (by Julie Evans, School of Architecture, University of Illinois, Chicago)

In the spring of 1984, I taught a studio at the School of Architecture, University of Illinois, where the students were asked to "redraw" the plan of Chicago as an architectural proposition. The project was based on a studio that Diana Agrest had taught at the Institute of Architectural and Urban Studies in New York during the mid-1970s, based on the notion of "design as reading." Students were asked to draw sequences of buildings or fragments of urban fabric that had not been architecturally conceived as such. The project consisted in developing a formal *parti* that was implied by the given sequence of buildings or urban fragments. The process was based on drawings that described only the pertinent elements while everything that did not relate to the architectural idea was "edited out."

By working with the *plan* rather than with *buildings*, this early study of urban form was based on the assumption that 'what we see is not necessarily what it is.' Freud's notion of floating attention, a process of visual drifting, suggested the search for symptoms, disruptions and discontinuities in the continuous spatial flow implied by the grid of streets of the American city, and in particular the plan of Chicago. The plan was approached without expectations, without knowing what we were looking for, to ensure that what was found was not that which we already knew.

While the neutral geometric grid and the regular "beat" of intersections in the city of Chicago imply continuous movement, the "accidents" of the plan produce changing rhythms, interruptions, stops and stasis. This led to one of the first discoveries of Chicago's underlying urban structure: the existence of a double street structure, where a neutral square grid of streets conceals a directionally biased structure of service alleys. The service alleys divide the square urban blocks into rectangular half-blocks, oriented sometimes along the north-south axis (parallel to the Lake Michigan coastline) and at other times along the east-west axis (perpendicular to the lake). This subdivision produces the reading of boundaries at the point where the service alleys change direction and therefore leads to the perception of a division between potential districts. A second discovery contradicted the supposed neutrality of the grid: the presence of an implied wall dividing north Chicago from south Chicago, white Chicago from black Chicago. This wall was implied from the fact that the monumental north-south axes seem to come to an abrupt end at the point where the streets change their name from north to south, marking a significant shift in the social geography of the city.
(see page 62)

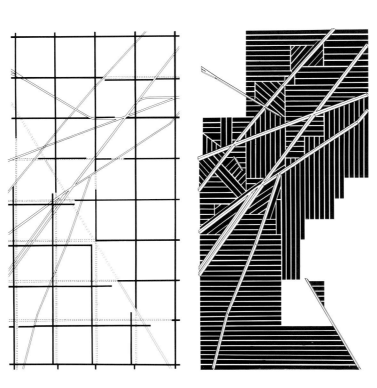

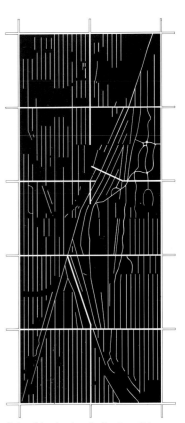

Series of drawings investigating the collisions, overlapping and fragmentation of the grid of Chicago
Drawings by Brendan Fahey (left and center) and Julie Evans (above), School of Architecture, University of Illinois, Chicago

Towards an American urbanism

The exploration of the plans of New York, Los Angeles, Boston and New Haven between 1984 and 1988 revealed in the American city a formal world ignored and obscured by both nineteenth-century picturesque and twentieth-century modernist European urbanism. The research aim was not the affirmation of a prior analytical "method" but to develop specific tools for different cities. This approach not only expanded the repertory of analytical tools and strategies but also suggested the possible development of a specific American urbanism based on the formal conditions uncovered by the analysis.

Some of the notions developed in previous readings formed the basis of a second studio held at the School of Architecture, University of Illinois, in 1988. While the plans of other cities or urban areas previously analyzed were rather chaotic, the plan of Chicago appeared as a basic grid. The earlier drawings focused on the notion of partial order implied in the collisions, overlapping and fragmentation between and within grids. In the drawings of Chicago, instead, the focus shifts to the distortions and disruptions of the grid, revealing the breaks in the one-mile grid produced by history (the diagonals materializing off Indian trails), or geography (the river and topographic variations). It was at this stage, as a fellow of the Chicago Institute for Architecture and Urbanism, that I decided to use the computer to generate a new series of drawings on Chicago. The possibility of working with the computer suggested a change of strategy. Instead of continuing the exploration of strong anomalies that challenge the order of the grid, I decided to look at the weak anomalies, the smaller disturbances that affect the grid.

The computer drawings: the frame and the quadrants

The computer analysis of the city of Chicago frames a 2 x 2 mile area which is an extension of the Jeffersonian one-mile grid that covers the territory of America. Framing is a "mechanism" defined by the computer screen which acts as a two-dimensional "cut-out." This "frame" can include the full figure of the plan or, through the zooming process, can highlight partial sections of a plan.

The selection and the location of the frame which defines four one-mile quadrants, were determined by two major factors: geography and history. Geography, in so far as the center of the four quadrants coincides with the point where the Chicago River branches towards the south and the north-west. History, insofar as one of the four quadrants is the original site of the foundation of Chicago. Thus, this process of framing the central area of Chicago produces four different quadrants which form the basis of the computer drawings series: quadrant 1 (the north-west

Chicago: the 2 x 2 mile frame of analysis

Quadrant 1	Quadrant 2
Quadrant 4	Quadrant 3

Chicago: the four quadrants within the 2 x 2 mile area

area, including Goose Island),
quadrant 2 (the north-east area,
covering the north of the Chicago
River), quadrant 3 (the south-east
area to the south of the Chicago
River covering Chicago's downtown,
the Loop and quadrant 4 (the south-
western area). The quadrants can be
seen to relate in different ways:
there is a shift from order to disorder
as one moves from quadrant 3
through quadrant 2 and quadrant 4.
and diagonally to quadrant 1. The
Chicago River is differentially related
to the four quadrants: its two arms
enclose quadrant 3, it dissects
quadrant 1 while it does not relate to
quadrant 2 and quadrant 4.

Aerial view of Chicago

The drawing series

It became apparent that this computer-based method for analyzing the "real" plan was an extension of the "peeling" process of the earlier "hand-made" drawings. With the computer this peeling, "de-layering," process becomes a major mode of operation. Layering is inherent to the logic of the computer. It refers to the simultaneous presence on the screen of two or more images, an electronic equivalent to tracing paper, where light "draws" the plan instead of pencil or ink. As a basic method for reading the plan of the city, "de-layering" suggests an inverse process to the process of design itself, where layers are overlapped rather than peeled away. De-layering discloses a "differential" system of urban notions, and forms the basis of the series of analytical drawings presented in this book.

The urban grid

These drawings allow conclusions to be drawn. The geometric grid is the basis of the American city plan, providing a support for urban forces to play and produce specific urban plans. As opposed to the unmarked geometric grid, the urban grid should be seen as a field of energy marked by geographic, historic, economic and cultural forces. These conflicting forces distort and fragment the grid and therefore stop the uninterrupted flow of movement implied in the geometric grid.

The "invisible" city

One cannot literally "see" a plan or a section in a building. However, architects can imagine or generate them as well as other readings of the building by means of the architectural apparatus of representation. One could go further in this process of reading and deciphering buildings through other explanations, such as the identification of a formal type or a particular syntactic development.

These drawings represent a similar operation except that the object is not architectural buildings but the city, a plural fragmented and scattered process that resists the architectural desire to reduce it to an object, to a consistent whole. The drawings do not literally look at the city.

They are not about building, but about plans. They are not the result of imagining or deciphering which only sets the stage for visual drifting to set in motion a process that unlocks the unconscious. It is a process which allows us to "see" certain formal configurations that are not perceivable in reality and, therefore, affects the way in which we see the city. The drawings actually produce a different city since we re-enter the city with different eyes. One could think of two cities: one before and one after the drawings.

The urban text

The drawings attempt to read the markings on the grid essentially at the level of the signifier. The articulation between the signifier and the signified, which occurs in a number of instances, is not the subject of this work. The different series confront the disorder of the plan from different perspectives implying that there is no way of producing a drawing that cannot be explained from a single point of view, one unifying story.

The different configurations, layers or sequences are constantly re-arranged by these different overlapping fictions. The plan can therefore be seen as a mechanism generating drawings and stories. However, this mechanism does not generate any story but *specific* stories which could be called *The Urban Text*, in this case the *text of Chicago*.

Should we be surprised by the fact that architectural form can be found in the plan of the city? Yes, if one considers the fact that there is no architectural intervention in the design of the plan. No, if one considers architecture as not just the practice of a specific form of "writing," but primarily as an art of "reading." It is the "reading subject," the principle that generates the architecture of the city by displacing its plan to "an-other" realm. The realm of the text.

Series 1

Basic Elements:
These four drawings
describe the basic material
used in the computer
studies of the Chicago plan:
the street layout, the
Chicago River, the one-
mile grid and the drawing
that results from combining
all three layers.

layer 1:
Chicago: the street layout

SERIES 1

layer 2:
The Chicago River

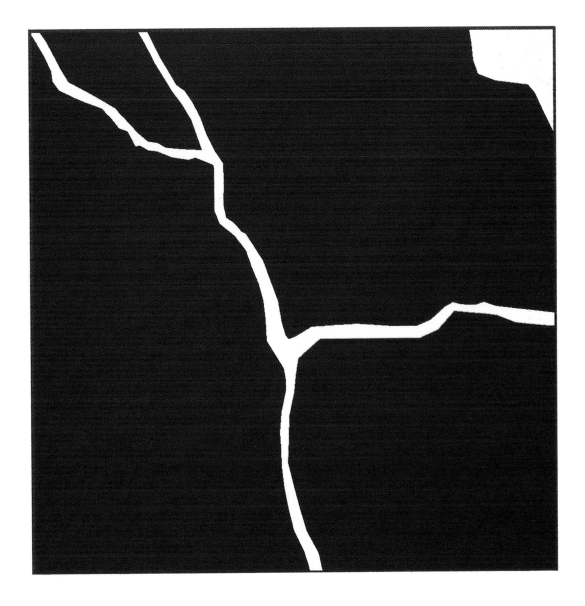

Series 2

The Four Quadrants:
These drawings present the
result of the first attempts
to read the plan of Chicago.
Although the eye is
immediately attracted to
the regularity of the grid
in quadrants 2, 3 and 4
as opposed to the chaotic
nature of quadrant 1, a
closer examination of the
'regular' area separates
quadrant 3, the 'Loop' from
quadrants 2 and 4. While
quadrant 3 is structured by
a neutral square grid, in
quadrants 2 and 4 the grids
are compressed producing
a sense of directionality.
A second reading of the
'chaotic' quadrant 1 reveals
a diagonal organization.
Finally, fragmented
orthogonal grids introduce
a contrast in quadrant 1
and disrupt the order of
quadrant 3.

layer 5:
Extensions of the directional
streets into quadrants 1 and 2
Subtraction of the true
regular grid in quadrant 3

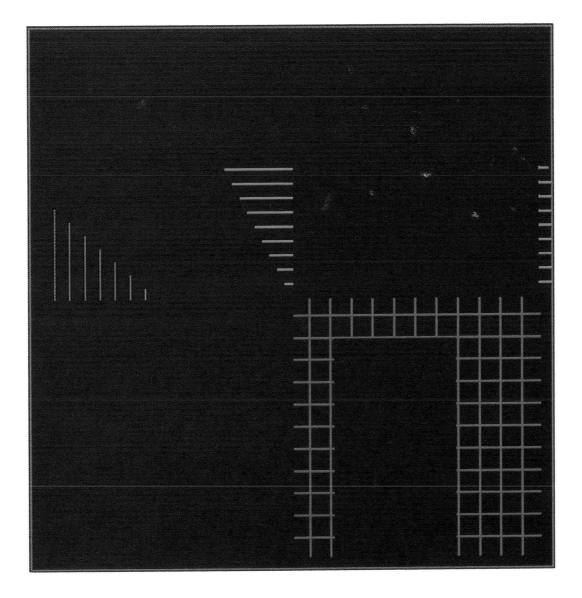

The Four Quadrants   layer 5 + layer 6
layer 6:
Anomalous streets in
quadrants 1 and 3

36

S E R I E S   2

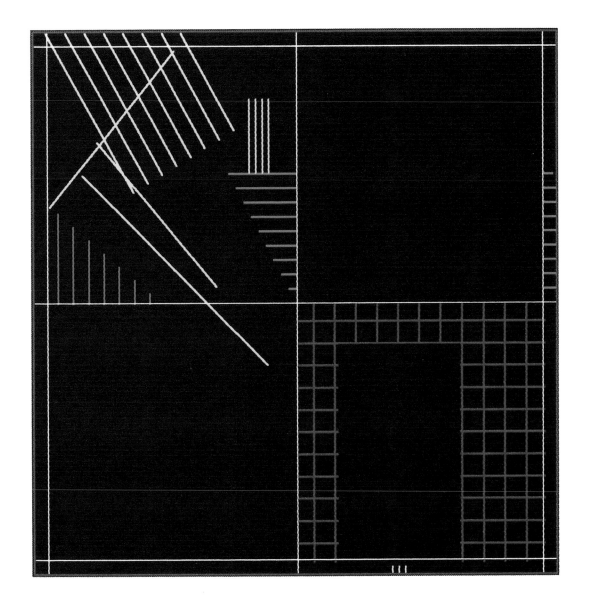

Series 3

Real and Ideal Grid:
The series describes the
ideal one-mile grid
and the actual location of
the streets that materialize
the grid. The drawings
reveal the minimal
differences that separate
the most abstract grid, the
(cartographic) one-mile
grid from the 'true' street
grid. The play of
differences cannot be read
in the 'reality' of the city.
The drawings are
indications of the dormant
symbolic potential of the
metropolitan scale yet to
be uncovered.

Real and Ideal Grid

layer 1 + layer 7 + layer 8
layer 7: the ideal half-mile grid
(dotted line)
layer 8: the real half-mile grid
(solid line)

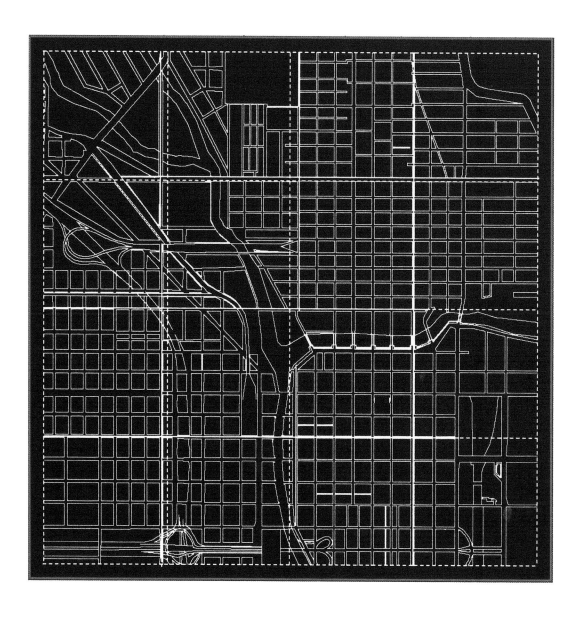

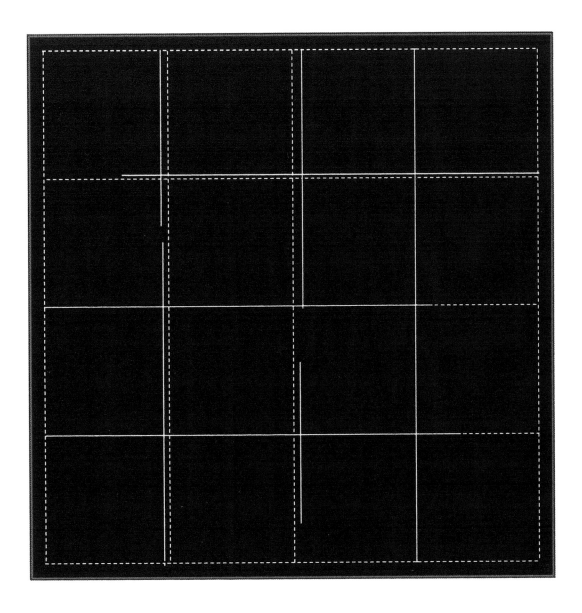

Series 4

Delayering:
The series describes
the four quadrants by
delayering: the horizontal
(east-west) streets, the
vertical (north-south)
streets, the diagonal streets
and the 'leftovers', all
those streets that remain
after the first three layers
have been subtracted. The
drawings imply that the
city could be seen as a
series of overlapping
formal layers with internal
consistency. They
represent not only an
analytical strategy but also
a potential design
mechanism.

Delayering

layer 9 + layer 10
layer 10: diagonal streets

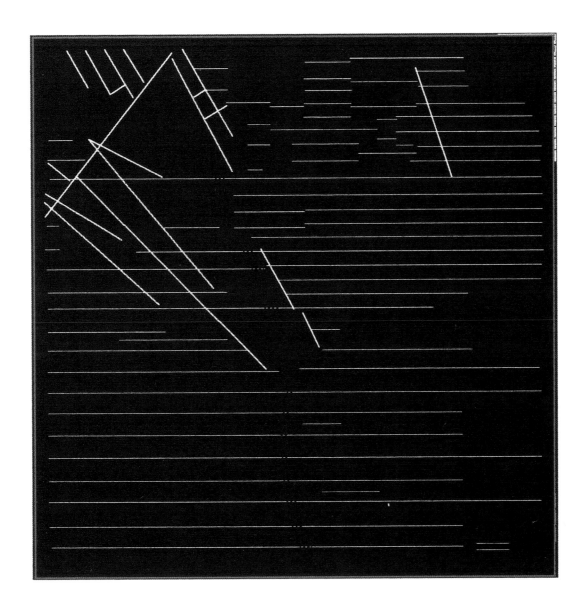

SERIES 4

SERIES 4

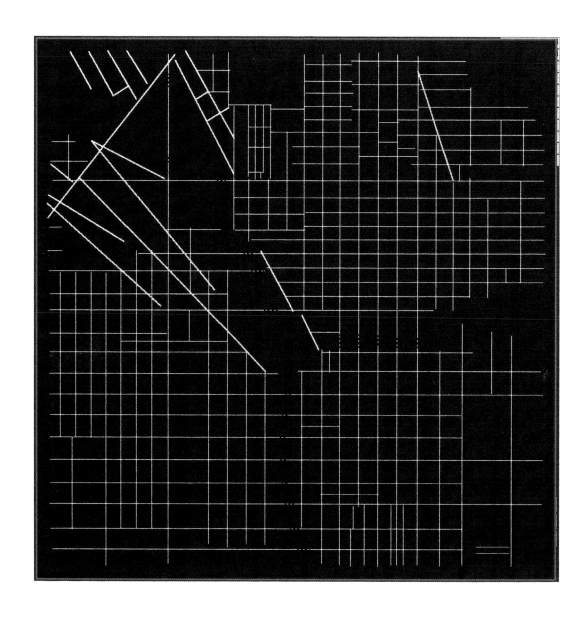

Delayering

layer 12:
layer 2 + layer 9 + layer 10 +
layer 11
The leftover spaces are
occupied by the Chicago
River and Lake Michigan

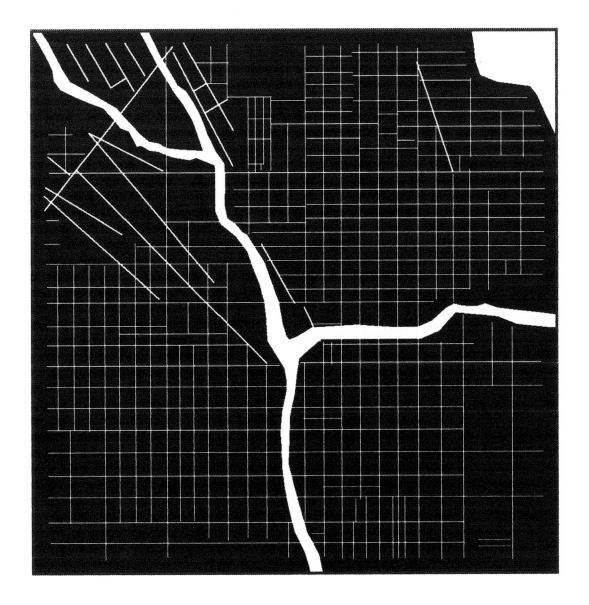

Series 5

Invisible Walls:
The series brings out an
element that is not
perceptible in the 'real'
plan: the 'invisible' walls.
The layers of the
horizontal and vertical
streets show in the breaks
or discontinuities of the
streets the "ghost" of the
Chicago River. However,
there are other breaks that
do not relate to the river.
Streets break implying
"invisible" walls that
fragment the plan and
produce districts that
coincide with the public
housing "projects" in
the north, or separate
black and white
Chicago in the south.

Invisible Walls

layer 9 + layer 13
layer 13:
North-South invisible walls
(red)

SERIES 5

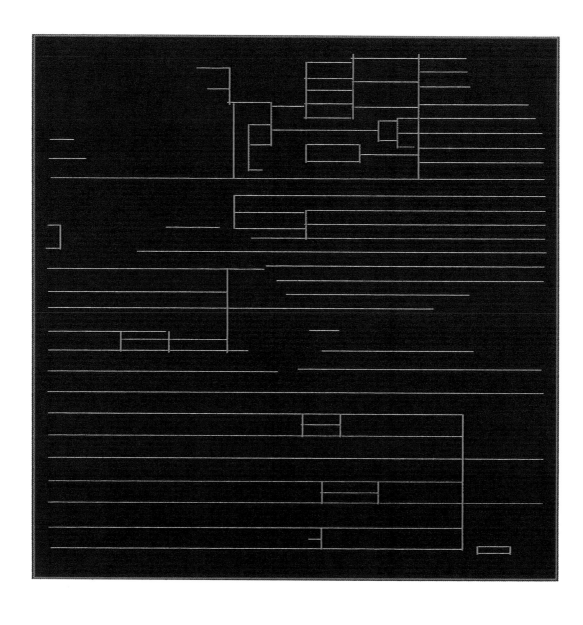

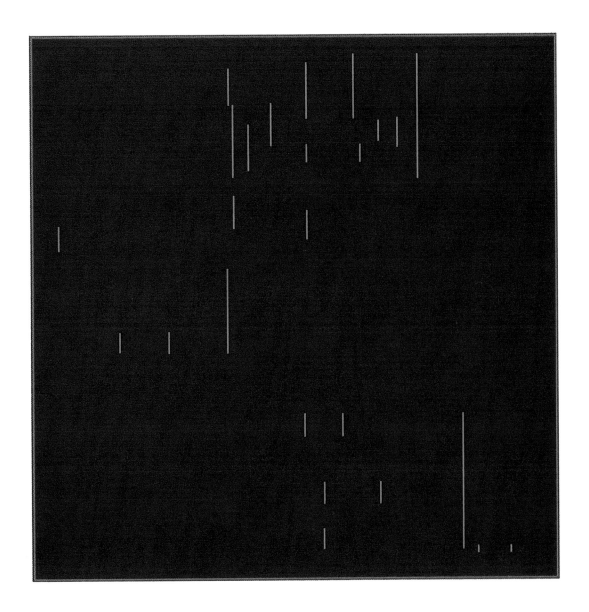

layer 10 + layer 14
layer 14:
East-West invisible walls
(green)

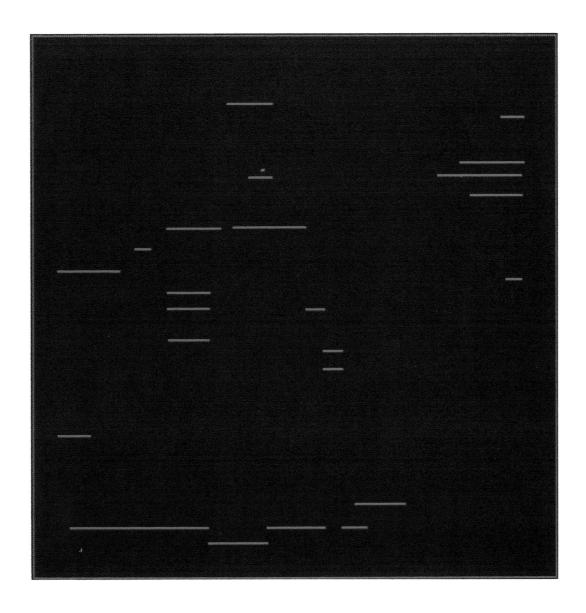

layer 13 + layer 15
layer 15:
East-West streets that stop
(solid lines) versus through-
streets (dotted lines)

SERIES 5

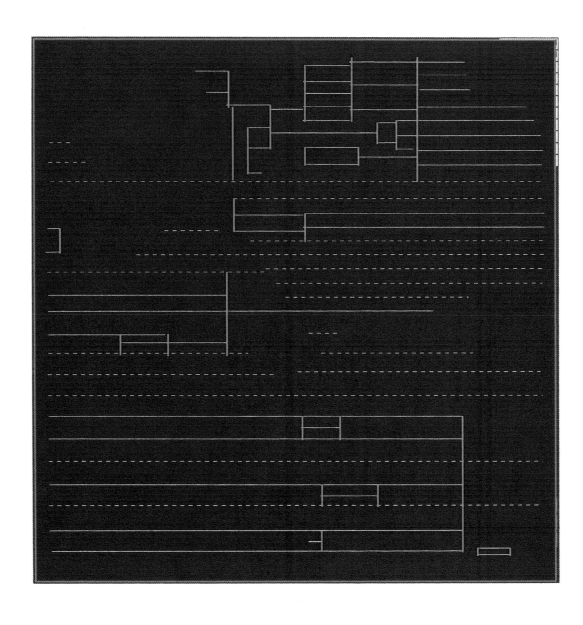

Invisible Walls layer 14 + layer 16
layer 16:
North-South streets that stop
(solid lines) versus through-
streets (dotted lines)

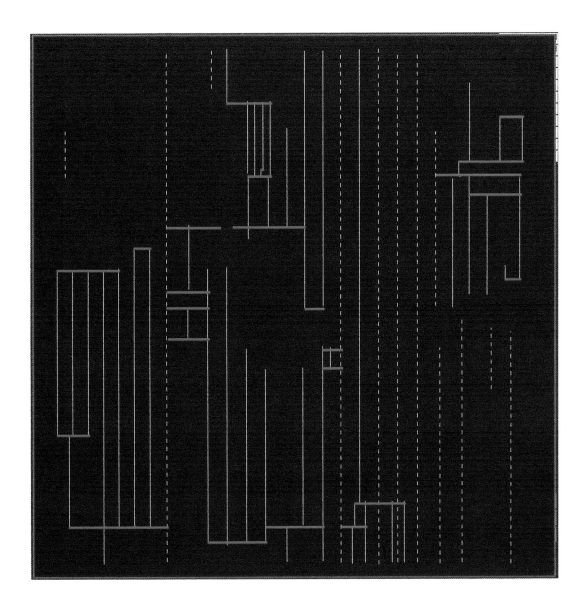

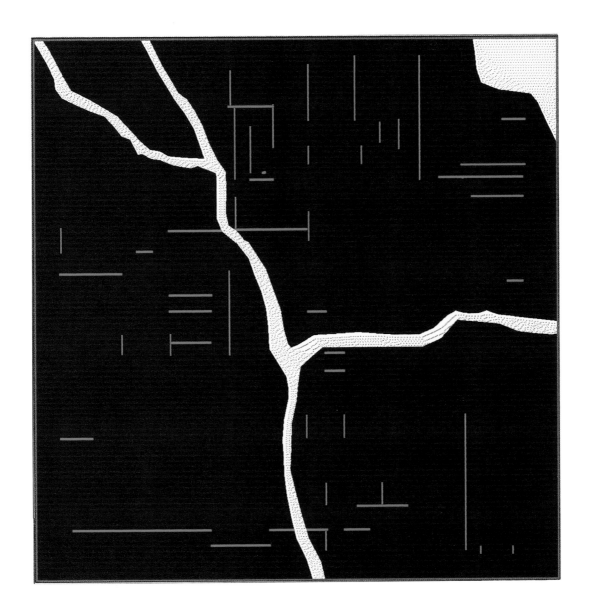

Series 6

Dead-Ends:
The series describes the
dead-end streets in Chicago
that play a symbolic role
similar to the monumental
axes in the European City.
However, in the gridded
plan of the American City,
the monumental axes do
not necessarily lead to the
expected monument-
Michigan Avenue slides by
the Chicago Tribune and
the Wrigley Building. The
monumental buildings
placed along the street
within the grid do not
interrupt the fluid linearity
of the streets. What stops
Michigan Avenue is the
fabric of the Loop, the
buildings sitting on its
gridded plan.

layer 2 + layer 17
layer 17:
Monumental buildings
and axes

SERIES 6

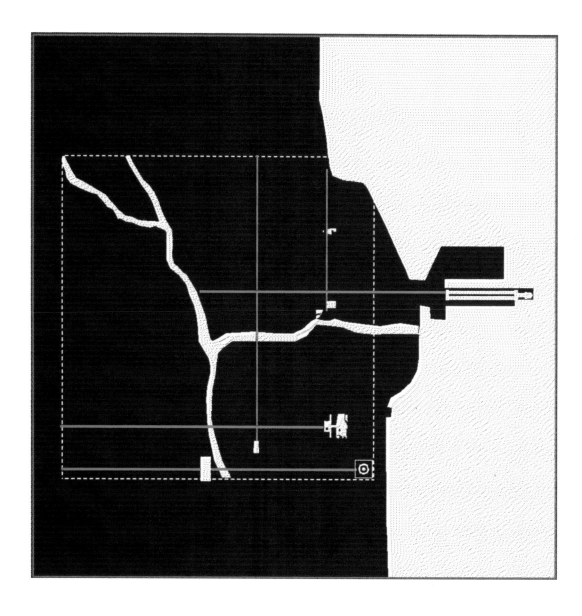

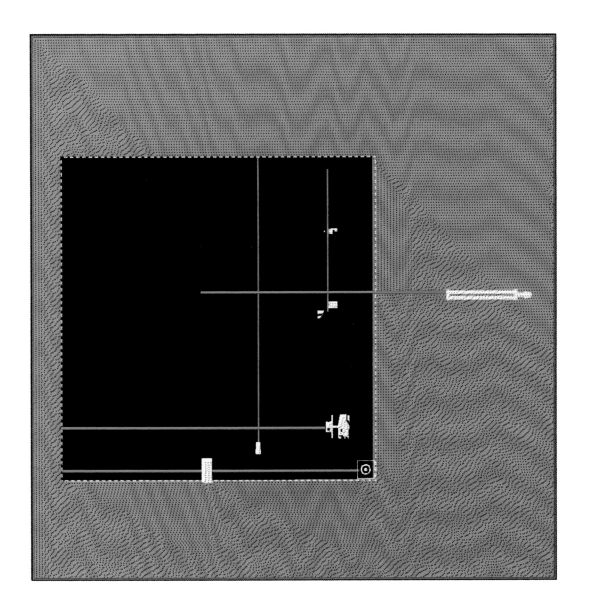

Series 7

The Foundation of Chicago: This series is a "graphic fiction". It tells a story in the form of a montage, the fictional development of the original plan of Chicago. It proposes a different strategy with respect to the previous series. The intention is to show that what the plan allows us to see at the level of perception is not exactly what it actually is and that it might be very different from its formal structure. The series describes a sequence of transformations and overlapping that proposes an explanation of the process starting with the geometric grid of the foundation of Chicago and ending with the present condition. The city of Chicago was in fact founded in the south-east area, in quadrant 3, framed by the two arms of the Chicago River. The streets of the original plan extended northwards and westwards. The sequence of drawings proposes a fictional formal logic which "explains" the displacement of the original grid, from its location in quadrant 3, westwards towards quadrant 4. It also "describes" the structure of the streets other than the ones related to the original grid.

SERIES 7

The Foundation of Chicago

layer 2 + layer 3 + layer 18 + layer 19
layer 19:
Extension of the original grid

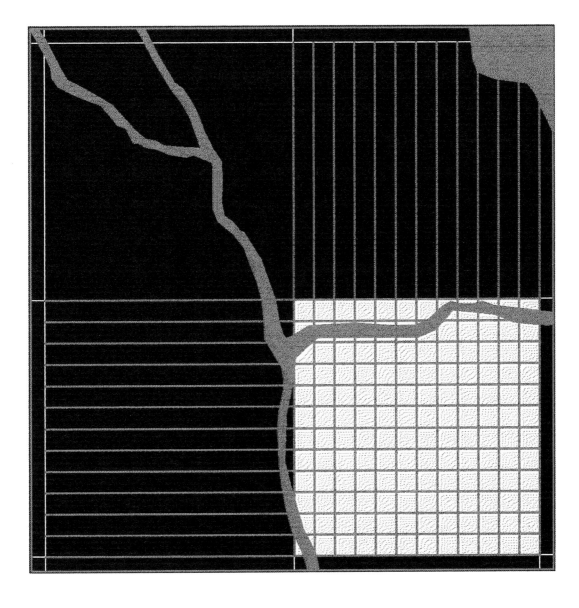

layer 2 + layer 3 + layer
19 + layer 20
layer 20:
Displaced 'original' square
mile to the original edge of
the Lake Michigan

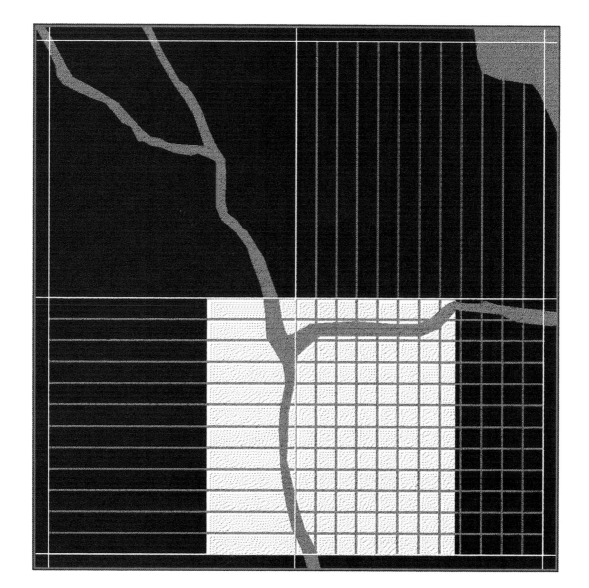

layer 2 + layer 3 + layer
19 + layer 21
layer 21:
The displaced original square
mile fragmented by the
Chicago River

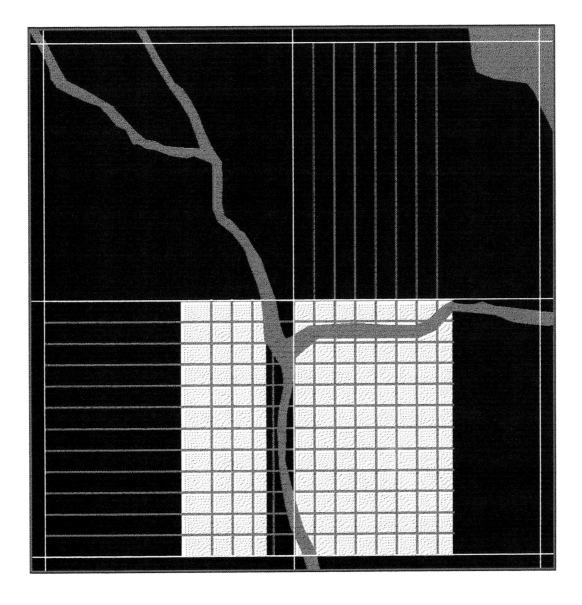

layer 2 + layer 22
layer 22:
Structure of regular streets
that coincide with the
displaced square mile

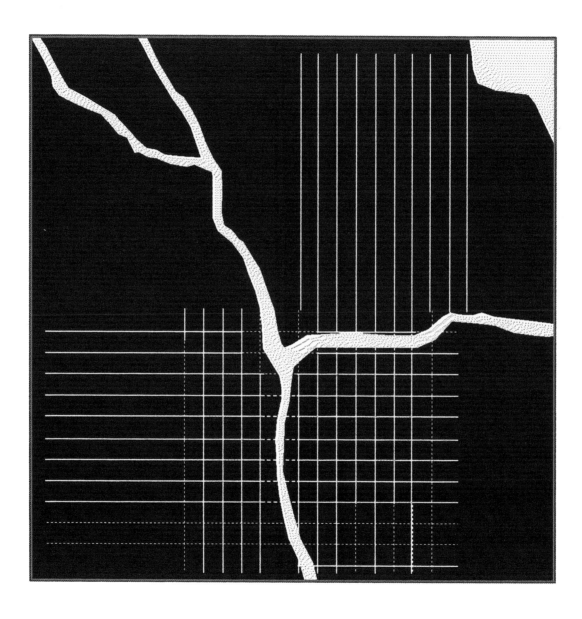

layer 2 + layer 23
layer 23:
Orthogonal streets that do
not coincide with layer 22

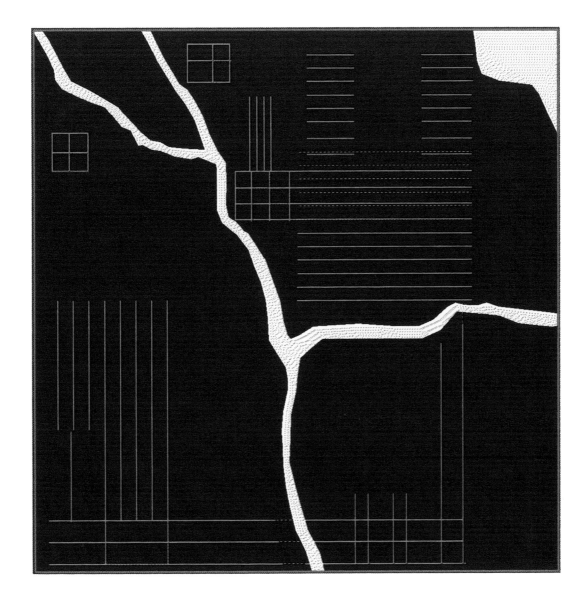

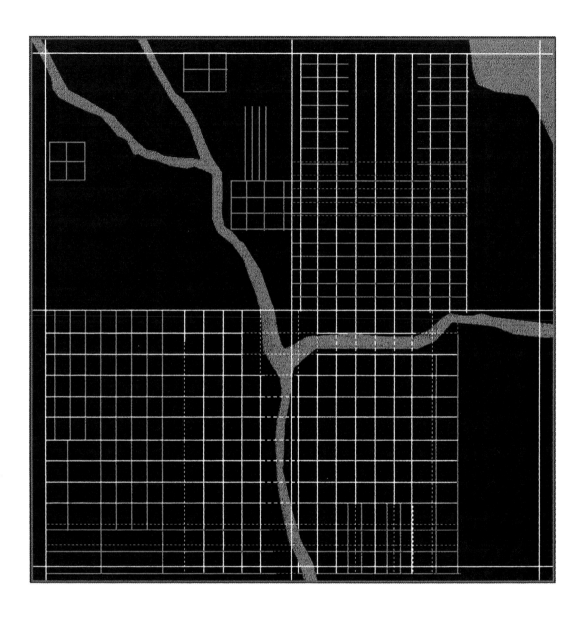

Series 8

The Reading of the Loop: The final series is the only one where buildings, or more specifically plans of buildings, are included. The Loop appears structured by a pure grid and an anomalous grid that "comes" from the south, penetrating the neutrality of the pure grid. The drawings point to the static character of the neutral grid in contrast with the dynamic character of the directional grid. The next question the drawings ask refers to the buildings in this area. Are they just 'fabric', or building-objects, or both? And how should they show the difference between the two conditions, between the extruded grids and the monuments? Fabric and building-objects seem to be the result of two inverse operations: while the fabric seems to respond to the forces of extrusion inherent to the grid, the building-objects seem to sit on the grid. A composition of lines and polygons describes the elements that escape the grid and its extrusion (the fabric). The polygons represent either building-objects detached from the fabric or extrusions of entire city blocks, which defy or neutralize the opposition between fabric and building-object.The lines represent the anomalous alleys that do not belong to the grid. They depart from the perfect regularity of the ideal model. The series proposes a reading where the buildings seem to belong to two different structures: fabric or objects on a field. It implies the notion of the Loop (and perhaps the American City) as a field of building objects overlapping the fabric of the city, or a twentieth-century city overlapping the nineteenth-century city.

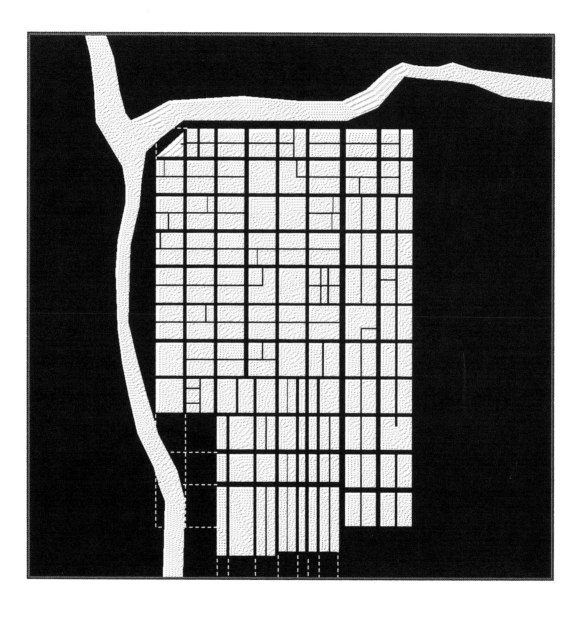

The Reading of the Loop

layer 25:
Formal structure of
anomalous streets and
southern alleys (red)

77

S E R I E S   8

The Reading of the Loop

layer 26:
Grid of streets and alleys in
the Loop (blue)

78

S E R I E S 8

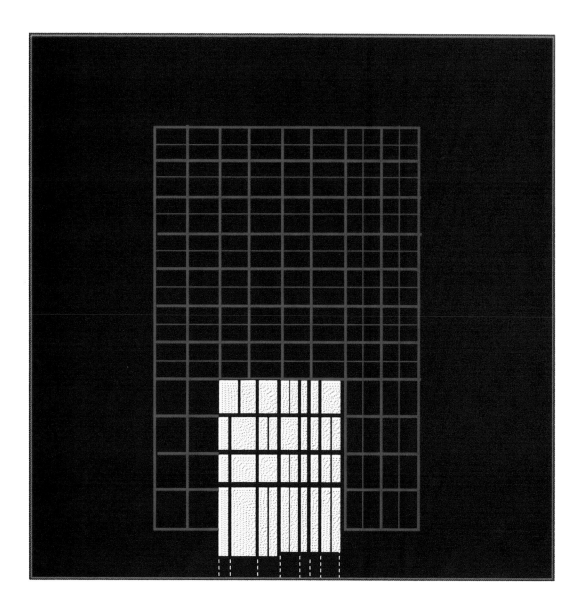

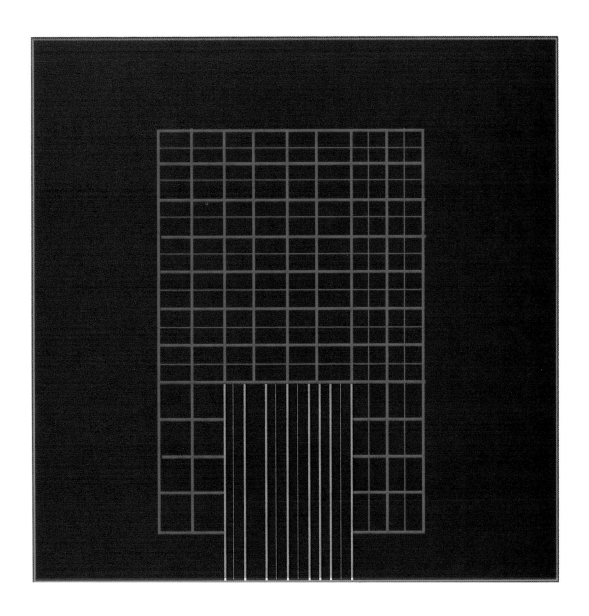

The Reading of the Loop

layer 25 + layer 26 + layer 27
layer 27:
Anomalous alleys (yellow)

80

SERIES 8

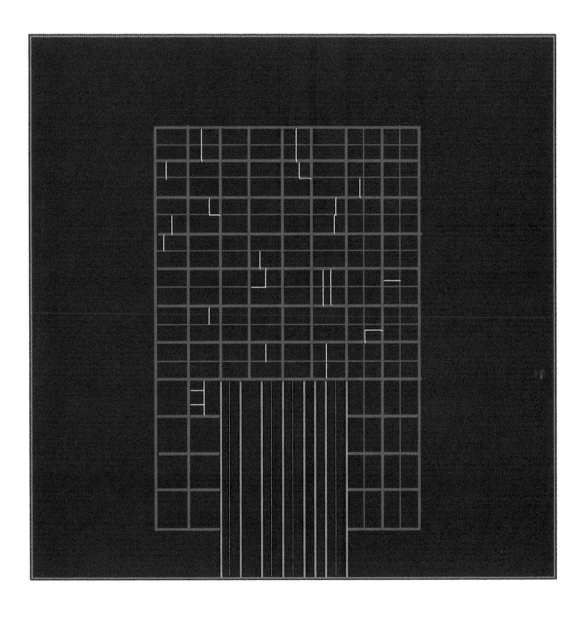

The Reading of the Loop

layer 25 + layer 26 +layer
27 +layer 28
layer 28:
Main buildings in the Loop

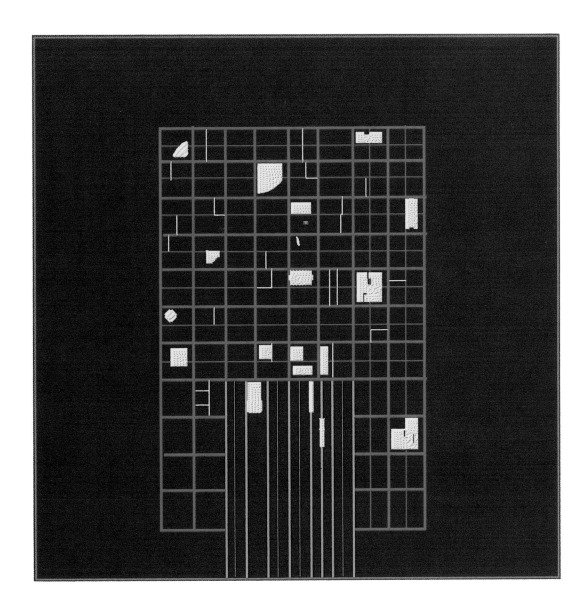

SERIES 8

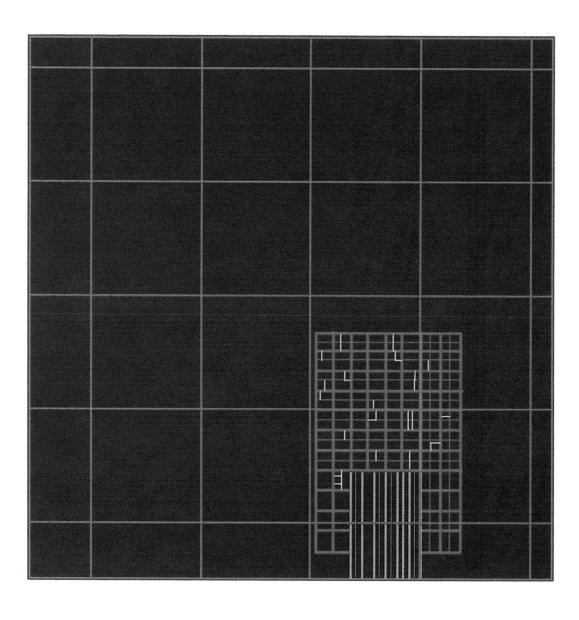

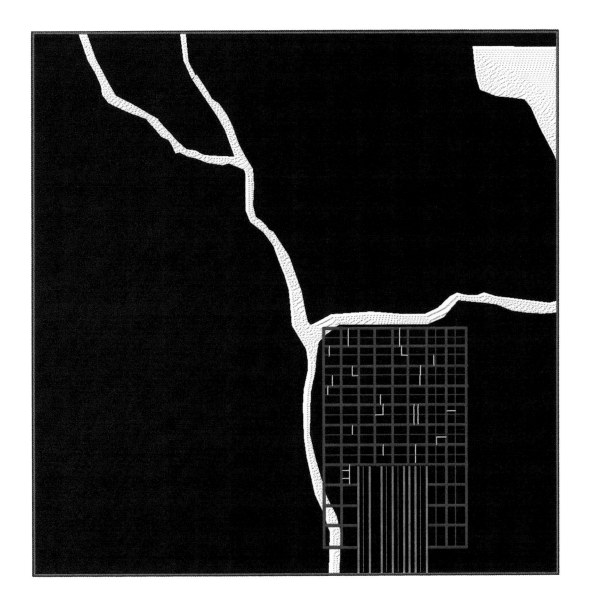

Series 9

Goose Island:
The orientation of Goose
Island (quadrant 3)
determines the diagonal
bias in quadrant 1.
Although apparently
discontinuous, the streets
can be read as fragments
of an implied grid. A
close-up view of quadrant
1 shows that the grids of
the adjacent quadrants 2
and 4 are discontinued
within quadrant 1,
transforming themselves
into a fragmented fabric
that can be read as large
objects in the field of
quadrant 1.

layer 2 + layer 10 + layer 29
layer 29:
Implied diagonal grid (dotted
lines) extending from Goose
Island

SERIES 9

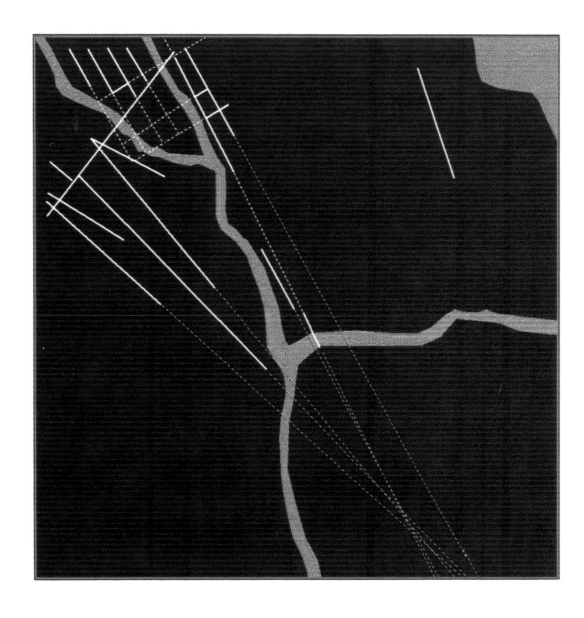

Close-up of quadrant 1
showing layer 2 + layer
10 + layer 11

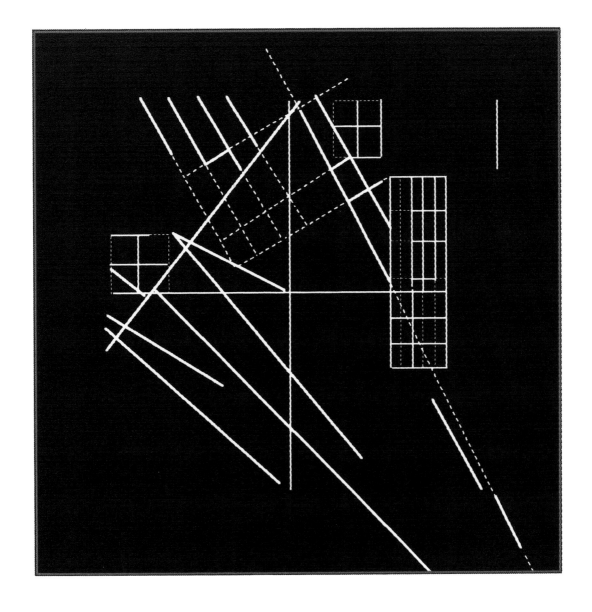

Series 10

City Views:
The City Views expose a
potential landscape that
results from the extrusion
of the diagonals and other
irregular streets and alleys.
The City Views represent
the 'other': the city of
voids (streets) as opposed
to the city of solids (blocks);
the city made by the
elements that remain once
the regular street-grid and
its transformations are
'subtracted' from the plan
of Chicago.

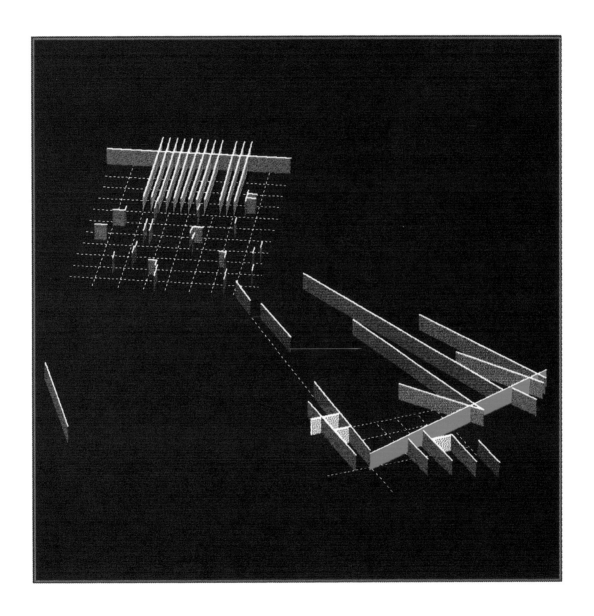

DATE DUE
